Clay County Public
Library
116 Guffey Street
Celina, TN 38551
(931) 243-3442

Tyler Perry

Other books in the People in the News series:

Tyler Perry

by Michael V. Uschan

LUCENT BOOKS

A part of Gale, Cengage Learning

Detroit • New York • San Francisco • New Haven, Conn • Waterville, Maine • London

LIBRARY OF CONGRESS CATALOGING-IN-PUBLICATION DATA

Uschan, Michael V., 1948-
  Tyler Perry / by Michael V. Uschan.
    p. cm. -- (People in the news)
  Includes bibliographical references and index.
  ISBN 978-1-4205-0309-8
1. Perry, Tyler--Juvenile literature. 2. Authors, American--20th century--
Biography--Juvenile literature. 3. African American authors--Biography--Juvenile
literature. 4. Actors--United States--Biography--Juvenile literature. 5. Motion picture
producers and directors--United States--Biography--Juvenile literature. 6. Television
producers and directors--United States--Biography--Juvenile literature. I. Title.
  PS3616.E795Z87 2010
  791.4302'33092--dc22
  [B]
                                                                        2010004744

Lucent Books
27500 Drake Rd
Farmington Hills MI 48331

ISBN-13: 978-1-4205-0309-8
ISBN-10: 1-4205-0309-X

Printed in the United States of America
2 3 4 5 6 7 14 13 12 11

Contents

ame and celebrity are alluring. People are drawn to those who walk in fame's spotlight, whether they are known for great accomplishments or for notorious deeds. The lives of the famous pique public interest and attract attention, perhaps because their experiences seem in some ways so different from, yet in other ways so similar to, our own.

Newspapers, magazines, and television regularly capitalize on this fascination with celebrity by running profiles of famous people. For example, television programs such as *Entertainment Tonight* devote all their programming to stories about entertainment and entertainers. Magazines such as *People* fill their pages with stories of the private lives of famous people. Even newspapers, newsmagazines, and television news frequently delve into the lives of well-known personalities. Despite the number of articles and programs, few provide more than a superficial glimpse at their subjects.

Lucent's People in the News series offers young readers a deeper look into the lives of today's newsmakers, the influences that have shaped them, and the impact they have had in their fields of endeavor and on other people's lives. The subjects of the series hail from many disciplines and walks of life. They include authors, musicians, athletes, political leaders, entertainers, entrepreneurs, and others who have made a mark on modern life and who, in many cases, will continue to do so for years to come.

These biographies are more than factual chronicles. Each book emphasizes the contributions, accomplishments, or deeds that have brought fame or notoriety to the individual and shows how that person has influenced modern life. Authors portray their subjects in a realistic, unsentimental light. For example, Bill Gates – the cofounder and chief executive officer of the software giant Microsoft – has been instrumental in making personal computers the most vital tool of the modern age. Few dispute his business savvy, his perseverance, or his technical expertise, yet critics say he is ruthless in his dealings with competitors and driven more by his desire to maintain Microsoft's dominance in the computer industry than by an interest in furthering technology.

In these books, young readers will encounter inspiring stories about real people who achieved success despite enormous obstacles. Oprah Winfrey – the most powerful, most watched, and wealthiest woman on television today – spent the first six years of her life in the care of her grandparents while her unwed mother sought work and a better life elsewhere. Her adolescence was colored by promiscuity, pregnancy at age fourteen, rape, and sexual abuse.

Each author documents and supports his or her work with an array of primary and secondary source quotations taken from diaries, letters, speeches, and interviews. All quotes are footnoted to show readers exactly how and where biographers derive their information and provide guidance for further research. The quotations enliven the text by giving readers eyewitness views of the life and accomplishments of each person covered in the People in the News series.

In addition, each book in the series includes photographs, annotated bibliographies, timelines, and comprehensive indexes. For both the casual reader and the student researcher, the People in the News series offers insight into the lives of today's newsmakers – people who shape the way we live, work, and play in the modern age.

A Man of Many Talents

Lots of people would love to work as an actor, playwright, screenwriter, theater director, film director, television director, film producer, or television producer. Tyler Perry has been a success at every one of those endeavors as well as several others. In 2006 he became a best-selling author with *Don't Make a Black Woman Take Off Her Earrings: Madea's Uninhibited Commentaries on Love and Life*, a humorous book based on the most popular character he has created in his plays and movies. And in 2008 Perry earned yet another title—that of mogul—when he opened Tyler Perry Studios in Atlanta, Georgia. A mogul is someone who is powerful enough to influence an entire industry. As the first African American to own his own movie and television studio and one of the most popular stars in movies today, Perry wields such power. He uses his studio to film two television series and the movies he writes and produces.

Perry explains why he has succeeded in so many different endeavors by comparing himself to a childhood toy. He says,

> I am like one of those building blocks that kids used to play with, where every time they turn it, there's another [letter of] the alphabet on it. So, every time you turn it [the block that represents his many talents] there's a character, a writer, or something else. And that's what I am, one of those building blocks. And that's [his versatility] on the bottom of all of this stuff [his success].[1]

Tyler Perry is a successful actor, writer, director, and producer.

One reason for Perry's success is the popularity of Mabel "Madea" Simmons, a character that first appeared in his plays. Madea (pronounced Muh-DEE-ah) is a large, boisterous, black grandmother. Her nickname is a contraction of the words *mother dear*, a term of affection African Americans from southern states in the United States use for older black women. Audiences love Madea because she is funny, kind, and wise. Perry plays Madea and is believable as an old woman, even though he was a young man in his twenties who was six-feet, five-inches (196cm) tall and muscular when he played her for the first time. The popularity of this outrageously funny character helped attract audiences to plays that had serious moral and spiritual messages, such as depending on God to overcome drug addiction.

The success of Perry's plays led Lionsgate Entertainment to turn one of them into a movie. Produced for just $5.5 million, *Diary of a Mad Black Woman* was a hit when it opened on February 25, 2005, and it eventually earned more than ten times what it cost to make the film. Perry moved to television with two popular shows, *House of Payne* and *Meet the Browns*, and on October 4, 2008, he opened Tyler Perry Studios in Atlanta, Georgia. Perry has written, directed, and starred in other movies as well, like *Madea Goes to Jail*, which was the nation's number-one movie when it opened on February 20, 2009.

Before Madea, movie deals, and television shows, there was a deeply personal project born of Perry's own painful childhood. Perry's successes started with *I Know I've Been Changed*, his first play.

A Play About Abuse

The play *I Know I've Been Changed* deals with a frightening subject—childhood abuse. Perry wrote the play in 1992 as a gospel musical with songs reminiscent of the Christian spirituals sung in southern churches. The play's theme focuses on Perry's deep belief in God and the power God has to help people overcome problems in their daily lives.

The play shows how Mary, a drug addict with two grown children, and her husband negatively shaped the lives of their children by subjecting them to verbal, physical, and sexual abuse. The children overcome the abuse and salvage their lives with the help of God. Perry wrote the play to make parents realize they must be careful in how they raise their children. He says, "I've been commissioned [by God] to help change a generation

Tyler behind the camera on his film Madea's Family Reunion. *Perry presented his first play in 1992 and grew into a major film star.*

through an anointed gospel musical called 'I Know I've Been Changed'. My orders are clear; show the people that being a parent is more than just being a provider. [Parenting is] an appointment by God to oversee the structuring of a human life."[2]

Perry also directed the play and played the part of a character named Joe. When Perry first presented the play in 1992 in Atlanta, only a few people attended. But Perry was so committed to spreading the play's message of hope for victims of childhood abuse that he kept putting it on in various cities for the next six years. The play finally became a hit in 1998 when Perry staged it at Atlanta's House of Blues, a popular venue.

Success from Misery

Perry knows about child abuse from firsthand experience. He was verbally and physically abused by his father and sexually abused by two other adults while he was growing up in New Orleans, Louisiana. The play *I Know I've Been Changed* is the result of Perry's own attempt to cope with his tortured past. "I started out writing myself letters to start dealing with the pain I've experienced as an adult,"[3] he says. Perry decided to turn the powerful lessons he learned while writing those letters into a play so that other people facing similar problems could benefit from them.

Perry continues to instill spiritual lessons into the plays, movies, and television series he creates. The moral elements in his work, from the love his characters show for each other even during painful periods in their lives to the power of their relationships with God, set Perry apart from most other entertainers. Perry says that the powerlessness he felt when he was an abused child has forced him to create works that can help other people. He explains,

> When I write stories with a message that says, "You don't have to take this; get out of that situation—there's a better life," it's as if that little boy in me is speaking, hoping my mother or somebody else's mother is listening. I know I'm speaking to a lot of people who can't afford therapy, who've never had therapy, and who see my plays and maybe "get it" in some sense.[4]

Chapter 1

A Difficult Childhood

On October 22, 2009, the CBS television show *60 Minutes* did a story on Tyler Perry's life. For the show Perry and reporter Byron Pitts visited Perry's childhood home in New Orleans, Louisiana. On the way there, Perry was nervous, and he told Pitts, "Man my heart is racing just being here, isn't that crazy?" When Pitts asked Perry why he was feeling that way, Perry admitted, "I don't have good memories here at all."[5]

It was not the neighborhood or his old house that scared Perry, but the things that happened to him while he was growing up there. Perry has talked often and openly about the many unpleasant experiences he had as a child, as an adolescent, and as a young adult. Perry once summed up his early life: "Lady luck wasn't kind to me in the beginning. As a poor kid growing up in New Orleans, my childhood was quite depressing due to poverty and physical abuse. I was the middle of four children. I was unhappy and miserable during the first 28 years of my life. The things that I went through as a kid were horrendous."[6]

Perry suffered while growing up because adults abused him verbally, physically, and sexually. The worst abuse came from his father.

Emmitt R. Perry Jr.

When Perry was born on September 14, 1969, he was named Emmitt R. Perry Jr. after his father, Emmitt, a carpenter and construction worker. His mother, Maxine, worked as a preschool teacher at the New Orleans Jewish Community Center. Perry has two older sisters, Yulanda and Melva, and a younger brother, Embree. Even though Emmitt and Maxine worked, the family was barely able to afford a home in a run-down section of New Orleans.

Perry's mother, Maxine, was his protector and friend growing up.

Even before his birth, Perry's parents had an unhappy marriage because his father physically abused his mother. When Perry was two or three years old, Maxine tried to leave Emmitt. She drove to California with Perry and his sisters to begin a new life. Even though Emmitt had bought the car for his wife, it was registered in his name. He reported the car stolen, and when his wife was arrested in California, he went there and forced her to return to Louisiana. Perry explains,

> My mother was arrested and my two sisters and I were put in the cell with her. He [Emmitt] and my uncle drove from Louisiana to California to get us. We spent several days in jail waiting for him. He bailed her out and couldn't wait to get her into the car. He got into the back seat with us and beat her black and blue from California to Louisiana, as me and my sisters watched. Even though I was only two or three, I know that this had to have some effect on me.[7]

The physical abuse Tyler witnessed on that long, frightening journey home would soon be directed against him.

An Abusive Father

Emmitt Perry soon abused Perry as well as Maxine, and Perry grew to fear him. Perry says the abuse was mental and physical. He recalls, "Growing up I never heard 'I love you' from him. I never got a hug, was never taken to a park to throw a ball around. Instead of 'How was school today?' I would be greeted with a backhand."[8]

Emmitt prided himself on his strength and endurance, and he had always worked at jobs that required hard, physical labor. Perry, however, was often ill as a child, and his father resented his son's physical weakness. Perry sometimes helped his father with construction jobs, but when Perry would try to saw wood, he would start coughing from the sawdust because he suffered from allergies and asthma. Those illnesses weakened him so much that he had to go to a doctor for weekly injections to control them. Even though his coughing was due to a medical problem, his

Tyler's father was verbally and physically abusive. He viewed Tyler's love of reading and writing, like this boy, as weak.

father would still belittle him because of his physical weakness. Perry says, "I was a disappointment to my father because I was sickly. I was allergic to everything, dust and mold. My room had to be cleaned [constantly to remove dust]. And I was always very tall for my body [skinny and not very strong]. The doctor used to say I was too big for my heart."[9]

Perry was also different from his father because he liked to read and do other things that required him to use his mind. His father, who had only completed school through the third grade, thought such activities were a waste of time and disliked his son because of them. "I [would be] in my room writing or drawing," Perry says. "That was too soft for a son of his—he would have preferred me to work on cars or do what he deemed to be manly things."[10] Perry says intellectual pursuits angered his father because of his own lack of education: "All he knew was the fields, the tractors and the mules and working with his hands, so here I come reading. Because I'm smart, you know, that was an insult to him."[11]

Emmitt thought his son was weak and needed to be toughened up. He did this by verbally and physically abusing him. Perry recalls, "He used his hands to pour concrete and hammer nails. He also used those hands to beat me. [He] thought he could beat the softness out of me and make me hard like him."[12] Emmitt also abused Perry because of the color of his skin. Perry is darker skinned than his father, which led Emmitt to believe he might not be Perry's biological father, even though one of Perry's sisters is as dark-skinned as he is. Perry says, "[The] other part of it [Emmitt's abuse] was my complexion. I'm darker than he is and he doesn't think I was his son. [I] have a sister who looks like me [but] she was very docile, so he never bothered her. But you know, I was the object of his disaffection."[13]

Other Abusive Adults

Emmitt Perry's hatred for his son grew worse the older Perry got and the physical punishments became harsher. "He threatened me," Perry says. "He would become physically abusive. Beating me with vacuum cleaner cords. Stomping on me."[14] One time Emmitt beat Perry so hard with a vacuum cleaner cord that he flayed skin off his back. Emmitt was drunk that night, and alcohol often fueled his rage against his son. In addition to hard slaps and other physical punishment, he demeaned Perry with verbal abuse and played cruel tricks on him. Perry describes the verbal and physical abuse his father subjected him to:

> "You F—ing jack—! You got book sense but you ain't got no mothaf—en common sense! You ain't——and ain't never gonna be——!" I heard this every day of my childhood. As my father would beat and belittle me, he played all kinds of mind games with me. He knew I loved cookies as a kid, most kids do. So he would buy them and put them on top of the fridge and when I would eat them he would beat me mercilessly.[15]

Perry's father was not the only person who abused him. When Perry was ten years old, he went over to a friend's house to play. The friend's mother later got Perry alone and sexually abused him. Perry also says an adult man molested him when he was growing up. Perry even experienced physical abuse from Emmitt's mother, who once gave him a painful bath in ammonia because she believed she could kill the germs that made him sick so much of the time.

It was a difficult life for a child and often his only protector was his mother.

Escaping the Abuse

Some of the worst times in young Perry's life were when his father came home drunk and vented his anger about life on his family. But Sunday was the best day of the week for him because his mother took him to church, the one place he felt safe and loved. Perry says, "You just never knew what hell you were going to get Friday or Saturday night. But no matter what, my mother got me up early Sunday morning. Nothing was going to stop us from going to church. That faith is was what kept us grounded."[16]

Perry's uncle, Reverend D.J. Campbell, was pastor of the church. It was during those church services that Perry developed his belief that God could protect him from all the bad things happening to him. Perry says, "My entire faith was born then, and my whole prayer life was based on if I just believed, things would be OK."[17] His mother sang in the church choir, and Perry developed a love for gospel music, which he has featured in many of his plays and movies. "The only time I really saw my mother smile," Perry says, "was when she was up there in the choir singing and happy. It's been very important to me, and it is stitched into my fabric. I love gospel music."[18]

Like many abused children, Perry dealt with his unhappy home life by using his imagination to take him other places where he could be happy. He says, "I conjured up other worlds: worlds in which I didn't worry about being poor, in which I was someone else's child, a child who lived in a mansion and had a dog."[19] Perry could even block out his father's shouting with his imagination.

During rough times, Perry found comfort at church where his mother sang in the choir.

He recalls, "[That's] where my imagination was born. When he was losing it and saying all those things [I] could absolutely be there in that room with him at the top of his lungs, and go somewhere else in my head."[20]

The young boy also had a physical place to which he could retreat when things became too difficult for him to bear. There was a small space beneath the family home he used to escape from his father. "This was my hideout, my safe place, you know," Perry says. "I'd spend all day in there. I had a door there so I could go in and close myself up, you know, to be okay for a minute."[21]

Perry also kept his mind off the bad things happening to him by reading, writing, and drawing. By age twelve, his drawing ability and interest in architecture enabled him to create plans for his

Memories of Abuse

On October 2, 2009, Tyler Perry sent an e-mail to fans that describes some of the worst incidents of abuse he endured as child. He was compelled to send the e-mail after seeing *Precious*, a movie about a young girl who was abused. Perry writes,

> I'm tired of holding this in. I don't know what to do with it anymore, so, I've decided to give some of it away…. My mother was out one night, as she loved to play bingo, and my father came home . . . mad at the world. He was drunk, as he was most of the time. He got the vacuum cleaner extension cord and trapped me in a room and beat me until the skin was coming off my back. To this day, I don't know what would make a person do something like that to a child. [His grandmother once said about his childhood illnesses:] "Ain't nothing wrong with that damn boy . . . he just got germs on him. Stop wasting all that money [on allergy shots]." When my mother left to visit some friends I heard what sounded like water running in a tub but it was sporadic. She [his grandmother] came and got me out of the living room leaving my Matchbox cars on the floor. She said she was going to kill these germs on me once and for all. She gave me a bath in ammonia [which hurt].

Tyler Perry, "We're All Precious in His Sight," TylerPerry.com, October 3, 2009," www.tylerperry.com/_Messages.

dad's construction jobs, and he even earned as much as forty dollars for drafting those designs. His interest in architecture led him to dream of becoming an architect. Perry never told anyone about his dreams for fear of being ridiculed. Perry says he knew he could not "share it with anybody, because they'll try to take it from you and snuff it out. That was the mentality of a lot of people I grew up

Writing To Escape

In a 2009 interview with a journalist from South Africa, Tyler Perry explains that writing helped him escape from the horror of the abuse he experienced as a child and kept alive his dream of a better life in the future. Perry recalls,

I had a horrendous childhood. My dad was very abusive—physically—to both me and my mother. [I] was quiet and always felt out of place my entire life. We grew up very poor, but somehow I always knew that I could have a better life. No one around me believed that. I ended up keeping my dreams to myself because whenever I'd share them with people they would end up tearing them apart. [I learned] to live my dream in a different form, through writing. And that is why to this day, I'm still writing. When I was a child, I would see the things my father did to my mother when he was still a dark and evil person, and it caused me to train my mind to go inside myself and go around the world to be in a happy place inside of my mind.

Quoted in Bonga Percy Vilakazi, "Talented Tyler," *True Love*, April 2009, p. 25.

around."[22] Even his mom did not encourage him to dream about his future. "My mother said to me, 'You are never going to make it, so stop what you're doing.' That was her way of protecting me [from disappointment or ridicule],"[23] recalls Perry.

Long-Lasting Effects

When he was sixteen years old, Perry changed his name from Emmitt R. Perry Jr. to Tyler Perry, the name by which he would become famous as an adult. Perry says he did that because he could not stand to bear the name of the man who had hurt him so much. "I just started telling people my name is Tyler. I didn't want to carry my father's name. I didn't want to be anything like him. I didn't want to be his junior. I have no idea where I got the name [Tyler] from,"[24] he says.

His father's abuse did take a toll on Perry, who became so depressed that he tried to commit suicide as a teenager by cutting his wrists so he would bleed to death. Perry talked about his suicide attempt once and said, "It was more frustration than anything, not wanting to be in that situation any more."[25] Perry still has a white scar on his left wrist that is visible when he does not wear a watch.

Perry says he was full of anger as a teenager and a young man and did things to hurt people, but has never talked in detail about what he did. "Listen to me," Perry told one reporter, "in my teens and twenties, I was hell on wheels. I wanted negativity. I thrived off it. If you tried to do something bad to me I could do it to you better."[26] In another interview, Perry admitted, "I did anything I thought I was big and bad enough to do. If I was hurt, I wanted everyone else to hurt. So I started building my life on unforgiveness and anger and frustration."[27]

Despite his sad childhood, Perry's intelligence and desire to learn helped him succeed in school. His mother has also said that it was in school that Perry first displayed his theatrical ability. "He loved acting, he loved to clown around with the children in school, but I never knew that it would [lead] to this,"[28] she said years after her son became a star. Perry did, however, drop out of Walter L. Cohen High School in New Orleans just three weeks before he would have graduated after having a disagreement with a counselor. He later earned a general equivalency degree (GED).

A lack of a high school diploma doomed Perry at first to a series of unfulfilling jobs, including carpenter's apprentice, waiter, bill collector, and car salesman. "It was a miserable time, but I was still believing in God,"[29] Perry has said. Even though Perry never lost his Christian faith, he was troubled by his past, especially the abuse he had suffered at the hands of his father. Perry was especially haunted by memories of his father telling his mother that their son would never be successful: "'One day that boy is going to make us cry. He ain't nothing and he ain't gonna be nothing!' These words found a place in my heart and have never been removed,"[30] Perry says.

Inspired by Oprah Winfrey

In 1991 when Tyler Perry heard talk-show host Oprah Winfrey say that people who have been sexually abused should write about it to help themselves recover from the traumatic experiences, he immediately followed her advice. One of the most successful African American entertainers ever, Winfrey was also a victim of abuse as a child. Winfrey first made the abuse public in 1986 on her show, *The Oprah Winfrey Show*. She admitted to millions of viewers that when she was nine years old and living in Milwaukee, a distant nineteen-year-old cousin raped her. The cousin then took her out for ice cream and told her that she had to keep what happened a secret, which she did. Winfrey was also molested by an uncle and a family friend. Winfrey has since used her fame to help fight child abuse. She also works to help victims of child abuse recover from their traumatic experiences. Her advice that day in 1991 resonated with Perry and led him to start writing about what happened to him, and it profoundly changed his life.

Oprah Winfrey and Tyler Perry are close friends who support each other's work.

Perry, however, always believed he could do something to make his mother proud of him instead of making her cry. Helping him in that effort was his desire to show his father that he could be a success. "Anger and frustration," Perry says, "made me get up and go to work every day to prove him wrong, while he kept saying that I would never amount to anything."[31]

Perry found the key to proving his father wrong after watching a television show.

Oprah Inspires Perry

In 1991 Perry watched an episode of *The Oprah Winfrey Show* that changed his life. During the show, Winfrey said that people who have had trouble recovering from bad experiences should

Oprah Winfrey talked about her own abuse on her show and inspired Perry to write down his experiences.

write about them so they can better understand them. Winfrey, herself a victim of sexual abuse while growing up, had done that herself. Perry took Winfrey's message to heart and began writing about his past. He explains, "I was watching the *Oprah* show one day, and she said it was cathartic to write things down. So I started writing all of this stuff down that I had been through as a kid, you know, from the darkest days to, you know, my father not thinking I was his child, and the abuse and the beatings and all this stuff."[32]

Perry found that writing did him deal with his past. What he wrote also led directly to his future success in the entertainment industry.

Chapter 2

A Play with a Message

On advice he heard on *The Oprah Winfrey Show*, Tyler Perry began writing about the abuse he endured as a child. He was especially haunted by his father's abuse and the hostile relationship he still had with his dad. Even though it was painful to dredge up such bitter memories, Perry says that writing about them eventually helped him deal with his past. He calls the writings "God's little flashes of light."[33] Perry used those memories to write himself a series of letters describing the events of his childhood and how he felt about those experiences as an adult.

Because Perry was afraid someone would find the letters and know the terrible things that had occurred in his life, he created characters who had undergone similar experiences to explain his tragic childhood. Eventually, Perry's fear about his deeply personal writings being discovered by someone came true. But when it happened, it turned out to be one of the best things that ever happened to him. Perry explains how that discovery started him on the path to success in his life: "I used different people's names because if someone found it I didn't want them to know that I had been through all of that stuff. So after writing all of this stuff down, a friend of mine did find it; he goes, 'Man, this is a really good play.' And I go, 'Wow, a play! OK.'"[34]

Perry had always enjoyed plays, and his friend's casual remark made him think that his letters could be the basis for one. Perry also began to believe that what he had to say about his childhood and his attempt to deal with the aftereffects of abuse could help other people

Gospel Musicals

I Know I've Been Changed, Tyler Perry's first play, is similar in many ways to other gospel musicals that African American theatergoers had been watching for decades. The plays written and acted by African Americans for African American audiences all share common traits. They are about the harsh things that can happen to people, have spiritual messages about how God can help people with such problems, and use comedy to make the plays fun to watch. According to *New York Times* reporter Campbell Robertson,

> The plays, which typically take place in contemporary settings, are often sprinkled with R&B solos and duets, and tend to be a mix between melodrama and farce, with clownish archetypes, like churchy grannies and two-bit entrepreneurs. And they all have uplifting plots, usually about a woman torn between a glamorous philanderer, whose speech is laden with double-entendres, and a humbler, more dependable man, whom she eventually chooses. (The more muscular actors also have a tendency to take off their shirts.)

Campbell Robertson, "The World of Black Theater Becomes Ever Bigger," *New York Times*, February 21, 2007.

dealing with similar problems. Perry told one reporter, "I realized that I had a story that would speak to an audience."[35] So Perry began writing *I Know I've Been Changed*, a play that would dramatically change his own life. That transformation, however, would happen in Atlanta and not Perry's hometown of New Orleans.

Moving to Atlanta

Perry visited Atlanta, Georgia, for the first time when he was twenty-one. Atlanta is a much bigger city than New Orleans. It also had more economic and cultural opportunities than

Perry was impressed by how many cultural and economic opportunities there are for African Americans in Atlanta.

his hometown and Perry fell in love with it. Perry explains the instant attraction he had for the city: "I thought I'd gotten to the Promised Land. I'd never seen black people doing so well. I'd always thought—because I tried to speak well and represent myself well, and that didn't go over too well with the fellas in the 'hood [New Orleans]—that I was crazy. But when I got here and saw other people doing the same thing, I said, 'I'm home!'"[36]

Many black people in Atlanta were more educated and had more opportunities for good jobs than their counterparts in New Orleans. Even though Perry did not have a college degree, he was intelligent and had learned many things by reading books. And by this time, Perry had also begun writing his play. He knew there would be more opportunities to stage it in Atlanta because more people in Atlanta attended plays. Perry was so impressed with Atlanta that he decided to move there. "I went back to New Orleans and [soon] loaded my

Hyundai and moved to Atlanta. I got a day job as a bill collector and scrimped and saved to put on my play *I Know I've Been Changed*,"[37] he recalls.

Writing a Play

By the time Perry moved to Atlanta in 1992, he had completed a rough draft of his play. The abuse that had marred Perry's childhood and led him to begin writing was the focal point of the play. *I Know I've Been Changed* is about two adult survivors of child abuse. The lead character is Mary, a drug addict who emotionally and physically abuses her son and daughter. Mary's husband also abuses the children and molests his son. The play's most important scene is when the adult daughter confronts her abuser and forgives that person. By forgiving her abuser, the adult daughter is finally able to shut the door on the past and begin having a better life.

Perry wrote the play as a gospel musical, a style of theater popular with African Americans. Gospel musicals combine comedy, drama, and music to tell stories that focus on how people need God to help them handle their problems. Some of the songs in gospel musicals are similar to spirituals African Americans sing in church. Other songs in such plays are more like rhythm and blues, the musical genre blacks created in the early twentieth century to reflect the harsh lives so many of them lived.

The title of the play comes from a famous spiritual titled, "Lord, I Know I've Been Changed," which repeats the refrain, "Oh I, know I've been changed, Woah I, know I've been changed."[38] The song, the first one in the play, sends the message that the singer would have a better life if he or she had a renewed faith in God. That point, as well as the need to forgive people, were the main themes of Perry's first play.

Producing the Play

Perry wrote a script for his play, even though he had no formal training in acting or writing for the stage. When he finished the script, Perry decided to use his life savings of twelve thousand dollars to stage the play at Atlanta's tiny 14th Street Playhouse, which seated only two hundred people. He paid for the use of the playhouse and the salaries of the actors and the behind-the-scenes workers who operated the sound and light equipment. Because Perry had so little money, he directed the play himself and took the part of Joe, an elderly alcoholic who provides comic relief from the dramatic, sometimes brutal events that unfold during the play. Perry even wrote the music and designed the sets, which included Joe's home, a hair salon, a diner, and a church. Designing sets came naturally to Perry because when he was younger, he had drawn plans for people who hired his dad for various construction projects.

When the play premiered in 1993, Perry had high expectations that his hard work would be rewarded. Instead, the play was a flop, and the failure hit Perry hard. "It was very difficult because no one believed in me. I used my own money to rent the theater, hoping that there would be a turn-out of at least twelve-hundred people over five days. But only thirty people showed up. So, I lost pretty much everything I had."[39]

The financial disaster left Perry, in his own words, "broke, broken and homeless."[40] The novice playwright, however, was unwilling to give up on his dream of sharing his thoughts about child abuse with people he believed needed to hear them. "I was determined," Perry says, "to see that show succeed, and I wasn't going to settle for anything less."[41] Driven to take his message that parents needed to love their children and treat them properly to as many people as possible, Perry tried repeatedly for the next five years to make the play a success. "It drove me and would pull me," he says. "What it ended up being was my destiny, it was where I was supposed to go, what I was supposed to do."[42]

Repeated Failures

Perry's initial attempt to stage his play had emptied his bank account, so he went back to work until he could save enough money to put it on again somewhere else. With financial aid from one of the few people who had seen the premiere of I Know I've Been Changed, Perry was finally able to put the play on again in

Trying to launch his play Perry ended up broke and homeless. For a while he lived in his Geo Metro, like this one.

another city. But when Perry took time off from his job to direct and act in his play, he was fired. This sequence of events repeated over and over as Perry fought to make his play a success.

During this period, Perry held some two-dozen jobs. And when he had saved enough money or received help from another financial backer, he would put on his play once again. Perry was able to stage *I Know I've Been Changed* about once a year in small theaters in Georgia, Alabama, and South Carolina. Perry was dismayed that his hard work was not being rewarded with success: "I tried to do this show for years and years. It kept failing over and over and over again. Every time I went out to do the show, nobody showed up. I was like, 'What is this about?'"[43]

Perry's life during this time was very difficult. He was always able to find jobs, like waiting on tables, selling cars or furniture, or collecting payment for bills. But the work was unfulfilling for someone who dreamed of being a successful entertainer and had a mission to help people deal with their own troubled pasts. Perry's various jobs did not pay much, and every time Perry staged a play, he sank deeper into debt. Eventually Perry could not afford a place to stay, and for three months in late 1996 and early 1997 he was homeless. Perry says he was so broke that "I couldn't eat. I was living in my car, with a friend, or at one of those pay-by-the-week hotels. It was a nightmare for me."[44] Years later, however, Perry was able to joke about his plight: "Can you imagine a six-foot-five man sleeping in a Geo Metro?"[45] he said with a smile to one reporter.

In addition to financial problems and physical deprivation, Perry experienced a spiritual crisis due to his play's continued failure. Perry's faith that God would always help him in difficult times had enabled him to survive his troubled childhood and given him enough strength to create his first play. Perry sometimes became angry at God when his play kept failing, but he says he never lost faith: "It was a miserable time, but I was still believing in God."[46] In 1998 Perry had another chance to stage his play in Atlanta. He went into the new production believing it was his last chance at making it a success. He recalls, "This was going to be my last show. I wasn't doing another play. I was twenty-eight years old at the time. I said, 'This is enough. You need to get a good job like your momma said and get you some [health] benefits.' [Even the] rent couldn't be paid."[47]

Finally a Hit

Perry rented Atlanta's House of Blues for yet another production of *I Know I've Been Changed*. On opening night, a nervous Perry talked to God about the play and his future, which depended on

The Fox Theater in Atlanta. Perry's play **I Know I've Been Changed** *was such a huge success that it moved to this bigger theater.*

the play's success. At first he began complaining to God about the play's repeated failures but then something miraculous happened. Perry explains,

[The] Spirit [of God] comes over me. I start crying. I got so calm. He said, "Look out the window." There was a line [of people] around the corner trying to get in [to the theater]. I thought, "Okay, this is bigger than anything I could imagine." I learned to surrender, which has been the most difficult thing I've had to learn in my life. Not my will, but His will be done.[48]

The Night the Play Succeeded

In an e-mail message to his fans that he posted on his Web site, Tyler Perry writes about the night his first play was finally a success:

> Anyway, the night of the play I remember sitting in the dressing room getting ready for the show. I was playing old man Joe at the time. I sat there complaining and talking to God saying, "You always get me out here and You leave me, and I'm 28. This is it! I'm not doing this anymore!" Can you imagine me talking to God like that? That's crazy! But I was so mad at Him then. So, I was saying what I wanted to say and in the middle of my rant I heard Him. IIIII HHEEAARRD HIIIMMM!!!!! Somebody knows what I'm talking about! He said to me, "I AM GOD. YOU DON'T TELL ME WHEN IT'S OVER. I TELL YOU WHEN IT'S OVER, AND THIS IS THE BEGINNING." I sat there crying like a baby. Then He said, "Get up and look out of the window." I got up and looked out and there was a line around the corner trying to get into the place! I still get a chill when I think about it. If I had given up on dreaming. . . . If I had not tried one more time.... I wouldn't be here in this place. I wouldn't have seen all that I'm seeing now. For that matter you wouldn't be reading this email.

Tyler Perry, "Try Try Try Again!!!" TylerPerry.com, March 5, 2009, www.tylerperry.com/_Messages.

Perry's show sold out that night. The play also sold all its tickets for its next seven performances. It was so successful and so many people wanted to see *I Know I've Been Changed* that Perry had to move it to the much bigger Fox Theatre, which seats forty-five hundred people. People who wanted to see his play filled the bigger theater for each show, and the play was finally a hit, six years after Perry presented it the first time in the same city.

The show's success in Atlanta helped Perry get bookings in theaters in major cities, like Washington, New York, Chicago, Philadelphia, and Miami. Perry toured with the play for the next three years, playing the part of Joe and directing the production. Wherever the play was presented, both Perry and the play got strong reviews. This review from a November 1999 performance at the Fabulous Fox Theater in St. Louis, Missouri, praised the show and especially Perry:

"'I Know I've Been Changed' is a hilarious show with a very religious message. Perry has scored a great hit and shown himself to be a performer of grand capabilities. Perry simply grabs the audience with his humor and then slips in his message of faith."[49]

After years of failure, Perry was finally a success both as a playwright and as an actor. But why it took so long for that to happen puzzled him at first.

Secrets of Success

As the play began to succeed beyond his wildest dreams, Perry tried to figure out why it was popular after having failed so many times before. He says the cast he assembled for his last-ditch effort might have been better than those of past shows. He had also learned more himself about acting and directing and made changes in the play which made it better. Perry also worked more closely with local churches, whose members were his target audience, to publicize his play and get the members to come to it. He even hired some pastors and members of church choirs for his cast.

All of these factors helped to finally make the play a success. However, Perry believes that the most important factor that contributed to its success was a change in his own life. "Maybe I visited the right churches. Maybe I finally got the word out," Perry says. "But until I die, I'll believe that when I finally forgave my father, the Lord blessed the play."[50]

Reverend T.D. Jakes approached Perry about writing the play Woman, Thou Art Loosed. *It grossed $5 million in only five months.*

I Know I've Been Changed is about an abuse victim who forgives her abuser, which helps her to be happier and have a better life. But Perry had never been able to truly forgive his own father. Before the play opened at the House of Blues, Perry called his dad. And during their emotional conversation, Perry was finally able to let go of the anger and hatred of the past and forgive his father. Perry explains what he believes that act of forgiveness did for him: "Doing the play enabled me to forgive my father and when I forgave him, every negative emotion that I had was released. That's when things changed—my blessings started to flow and the success came."[51]

The show's success helped Perry deal with his past and paved the way for a brighter future. In the years Perry struggled to make his play a success, people in the entertainment business had rejected his pleas for help. But once the play was a hit, those same people were suddenly interested in it. Perry says,

Forgiving His Father

Tyler Perry believes his play *I Know I've Been Changed* finally became a success in 1998 because he was finally able to forgive his father for abusing him as a child. In an interview more than a decade later, Perry explains how it happened:

[In 1998] I had an argument with my father. I was screaming and yelling and using every four-letter word in the book; I was twenty-eight years old and as profane as I could be. But I got an opportunity to have my catharsis on the phone. After it was over, I was empty, and I went on this journey to find out what was ripped away. And of course any journey for me is going to begin with faith, begin with God. I didn't pray immediately, because I was angry with God, angry with everybody. But remembering everything I had learned in church really helped me to get through that anger. I had accepted the words I had written [in the play about forgiveness]; I had forgiven my father. The show wasn't hypocritical anymore. It was coming from a very real place. And it started to resonate with people on a different level.

Quoted in Nina Hämmerling Smith, "The Power of Forgiveness: Letting Go of His Painful Past Made Tyler Perry a Superstar," *Guideposts*, February, 2009, www.guideposts.com/story/tyler-perry-power-forgiveness.

"After the show [became a success], every person who had told me no, every promoter who had turned me down, came to me with an offer."[52]

One of the offers was from Reverend T.D. Jakes, who asked Perry to help him create a play titled *Woman, Thou Art Loosed*. Jakes is pastor of the Potter's House, a church in Dallas, Texas, with thirty thousand members. He is also the host of a television show and the author of more than thirty books. *Woman, Thou Art Loosed* is based on one of his books by the same name. The book deals with many of the same topics in Perry's play, such as the sexual abuse of a twelve-year-old girl. Perry helped Jakes write the script for the play, and when it opened in 1999, it grossed more than $5 million in only five months.

New Opportunities

The success of *I Know I've Been Changed* and *Woman, Thou Art Loosed* changed Perry's life. The plays cemented his status as a prominent new playwright and gave him opportunities to write more plays and to eventually branch out into film and television. The money Perry made on those first two plays also rescued him from a life of poverty that had included being homeless. Perry, however, did not care as much about the money as the new opportunities he had to use his work to help other people. As a child, Perry had been powerless to protect his mother or himself from his father's abuse. His goal with the play and his other works has always been to show people in similar situations that there is hope that they themselves can escape such misery.

Chapter 3

A Successful Playwright

In the decade after *I Know I've Been Changed* finally became a hit, Tyler Perry wrote, directed, and often starred in ten more plays. His works were usually performed six times a week in small theaters in the South and in big cities like New York, Chicago, and Los Angeles. Perry's plays were very popular and each week took in between $250,000 and $300,000 in ticket sales, making him famous and comfortably rich.

According to Ashton Springer, a respected commentator on African American theater, Perry is successful because he gives his audience what it wants. Springer explains, "His plays hit the spot of what appeals to a segment of the black community who can identify with some of the characters being portrayed onstage."[53] Perry does this by sticking to the formula that made his first play successful. His plays all have strong Christian and moral messages and plots that show how people with problems, like drug addiction or sexual abuse, can overcome them. They also have rousing gospel and rhythm-and-blues songs and healthy doses of comic relief from the harsh and tragic scenes.

In *I Know I've Been Changed* the character of Joe, the comical old man Perry played, generates most of the laughs by making rude jokes about his physical ailments. In Perry's second solo play, *I Can Do Bad All by Myself* (2000), it is Joe's sister who steals the show. Her name is Mabel Simmons, whose nickname is Madea, and she became one of Perry's most enduring characters. One reason she is so memorable is that the 6-foot, 5-inch

Tyler Perry Becomes Madea

I Can Do Bad All by Myself is the play that introduced Mabel "Madea" Simmons, Tyler Perry's most famous character. Perry is 6-feet, 5-inches (196cm) tall, and he is bulked up by a padded fat suit when playing Madea, so she is a commanding presence onstage. When the play premiered in Chicago, Illinois, Perry was

Perry wears a padded fatsuit as Madea.

extremely nervous, because it was the first time he would be onstage dressed as a woman, and he did not know if the audience would accept a young man playing an old woman. Perry explains the feelings he had before that first performance:

> It was Madea's first time on stage, I was scared to death. It was the Regal Theater, 79th and Stony Island. I had rehearsed all month [for] the show without ever looking at a costume or putting it on. The night of the show I put the costume on and looked at myself and was like, "Oh god, what have I gotten myself into? It's sold out there and these people are waiting." So I'm standing there and they're saying, "Go, go, go," and Brown [actor David Mann who plays Mr. Brown] pushed me on stage. And that's where she was born.

Quoted in Brad Balfour, "Tyler Perry Discusses I Can Do Bad All by Myself," Huffington Post, September 23, 2009, www.huffingtonpost.com/brad-balfour/media-mogul-tyler-perry-d_b_295870.html.

Perry portrays her by donning a scraggly gray wig, oversize glasses, a huge billowing dress, and a fat suit complete with jumbo breasts.

Madea Is Born

The word *madea* is a southern black term for "Mother Dear." When Perry was trying to think of a funny character to add humor to his second play, he decided to create a wild and wacky but also wise and lovable grandmother figure. The character represents the many strong, older women he knew as a child in New Orleans. Perry says, "She's the type of grandmother that was on every corner when I was growing up. She smoked. She walked out of the house with her curlers and her muumuu and she watched everybody's kids. She didn't take no crap. She's a strong figure where I come from. [In my childhood] this woman was very, very visible."[54]

Perry patterned the character Madea after his mother's (right) tenderness, and his Aunt Mayola's (left) humor.

Perry did not have to search far for inspiration for his new character's personality. He patterned her after his mother, Maxine, and his aunt, Mayola. Perry says, "The nurturing part of Madea comes from my mother, who would open the doors of our home to you no matter who you were. My aunt inspired the pistol-packing, the wig and the voice."[55] Madea does carry pistols in her purse, and in almost every play she pulls one out and starts shooting; somehow, though, Madea never hits anybody and the audience knows it is all in fun. In her debut appearance Madea delivers a line that sums up her flamboyant personality: "I am six feet tall, sixty-eight years old, and 392 pounds. I can say what I want to say and nobody can stop me."[56]

In the play Madea's granddaughter, Vianne, moves into her home to escape her cheating, abusive husband, who is divorcing her. The play also focuses on a second granddaughter, Maylee, and her fourteen-year-old daughter, Keisha, who also live with Madea. The complicated plot has many twists, including the discovery that Keisha is pregnant. When Madea learns about the pregnancy she sternly tells Keisha, "You goin' to school, goin' to college, and you goin' to take care of that child. You not gonna be like your momma."[57]

In her own rough way, Madea loves the young girl and is trying to help her deal with a serious problem. And Perry believes Madea's dramatic antics are key to getting people into the theater so he can spread the spiritual messages he embeds in his plays. He explains, "I know Madea is a ridiculous character. But she invites the audience in to get a message across. I can talk about forgiveness. I can talk about being there for your family. Let that sink in for a second and here comes something silly to bring you out of it. This has all been an experiment. And the experiment is working."[58]

Madea first hit the stage at the Regal Theater in Chicago, Illinois. Perry was scared the first time he played the part because he feared the audience would reject a man wearing a wig, dress, and fat suit. But the audience loved Madea, and she quickly became the centerpiece of Perry's burgeoning career as the nation's most popular African American playwright.

Madea is always ready to set things straight, whether by a frying pan or with the pistol kept in her purse.

Perry the Playwright

Most people who want to write plays usually take classes to learn how to write them, and they gain practical experience by working for theatrical productions. But Perry's first play grew so quickly out of his therapeutic writings about his childhood abuse that he did not have time to learn how to write a play. And he is glad he never had formal training in writing. Perry explains, "Ignorance is truly bliss. If I had learned the structure of what theater is, I don't think it would have worked for me because I have to be totally free in my writing, totally free in my acting, totally free [to talk] to the audience. Because all of that makes the Tyler Perry experience."[59]

A hilarious example of Perry talking directly to the audience occurred when he was performing in a play in New York after the terrorist attacks on the United States on September 11, 2001. When people who arrived late started arguing with other people while trying to find their seats, Madea chastised them from the stage saying, "The only person y'all need to be

Actor David Mann plays Madea's neighbor Mr. Brown. Meet the Browns was a successful play and movie.

fighting is Osama! Git somewhere and sit down!"[60] The joking reference to terrorist leader Osama bin Laden stopped the disturbance and made everyone laugh. And when two of the characters in the play *Madea Goes to Jail* (2005) decide to get married, Madea says she knew all along they would marry each other. When Madea is asked how she knew, she replies coyly, "How? I wrote it,"[61] a sly reference to Perry's authorship of the play.

How Tyler Perry Writes

People who write works of fiction all have their own unique ways of dreaming up characters and story lines. Tyler Perry creates characters like Mabel "Madea" Simmons by talking to himself about what he wants to write. Perry claims that the characters he invents actually begin talking back to him. He explains,

> How do I come up with all these characters for these shows? I'm a little psycho and I sit around the house and I talk to myself until ideas come. The story lines for these plays usually come from thoughts. What I'll do is develop them and see them through and hear all these different voices in my head talking. I can actually sit in a room and hear these people having conversations around me. That's how I write. Somebody will be saying something crazy and then I'll hear Madea. Writing for Madea was actually pretty easy for me because the Madea character always comes last. What I do is I'll write the story first and then go back and add all the Madea dialogue. She kind of dictates to me what she wants to say in every situation. It's a very, very natural process for me to write that way.

Tyler Perry, "Special Features," *Meet the Browns* (play), DVD, directed by Tyler Perry. Santa Monica, CA: Lionsgate Home Entertainment, 2008.

Perry also allows himself and other actors in his plays the freedom to say things spontaneously because he believes improvising helps actors avoid boredom and brings new life to the production. Perry banters the most with actor David Mann, who plays the role of Mr. Brown, Madea's short, fat, bald, next-door neighbor. Brown draws laughs just by coming on stage in his wildly colorful, crazily mismatched outfits. And his personality is almost as outrageous as that of Madea, who taunts Brown every time she sees him.

An example of the ad-libbing Perry allows occurred in a scene from *Meet the Browns* (2004), a play Perry wrote, directed, and produced but did not act in. Mann's real-life wife, Tamela, plays the role of Cora, Madea's daughter. In one scene Cora went into the kind of angry rage Madea has made famous in other plays, waving her arms and then pulling a gun from her purse. The audience thought the takeoff on Madea was hilarious. So did Perry, who told Tamela to keep the ad-lib in the show. Perry says, "It's always funny to see the audience reaction to that because they know that is totally Madea. And for her to do it, that was an ad-lib one night. I was sitting in the audience and when she did it I almost fell under the chair I thought it was so funny."[62]

The loose, casual nature of Perry's productions creates a joyous, partylike atmosphere and it is what makes fans love the plays so much. Perry's approach is different from the formal approach of big-budget plays that make it to Broadway, the New York theater district that is considered the pinnacle of theatrical success. Perry's plays are better suited for what is known as the Urban Theater Circuit. These are smaller theaters throughout the nation that feature productions aimed at African Americans.

The Urban Theater Circuit

During the period of racial discrimination and segregation in the United States from the end of the Civil War to the 1960s, the Urban Theater Circuit was commonly called the Chitlin' Circuit. The name comes from chitterlings, a popular southern soul food. Theaters on the Chitlin' Circuit were often the only ones in which black entertainers were allowed to perform. W.E.B. Du Bois, one

Perry first appeared as Madea at the famous Regal Theatre in Chicago.

of the early twentieth century's most prominent civil rights leaders, once said this circuit of theaters was "for us, by us, about us, and near us."[63] One of its most famous venues is the Regal Theater in Chicago, where Perry first appeared as Madea. Many famous black entertainers, like the Jackson 5 with Michael Jackson, B.B. King, Ray Charles, Richard Pryor, the Supremes, and Tina Turner, got their start on this circuit before gaining greater fame with mixed audiences.

The Chitlin' Circuit, now more commonly called the Urban Theater Circuit, still exists for entertainment aimed at black audiences, including plays like the ones Perry writes and stars in. Perry made tens of millions of dollars with his plays, and he was considered the circuit's top playwright. Despite that, Perry was still relatively unknown outside the African American community until he started making movies based on his plays. In a 2009 interview Perry acknowledged, "I was able to build and have this amazing career among my own people [African Americans], but outside of that, you know, not a lotta people knew who I was."[64]

Although Perry's plays are popular, some African Americans have criticized him for the characters he created. Gary Anderson, founder of Detroit, Michigan's respected Plowshares Theatre, claims Madea and some of Perry's other characters are negative black stereotypes that debase African Americans. Anderson even compared Perry's plays to *The Amos 'n' Andy Show*, a 1950s television show about blacks that many African Americans found demeaning. But Woodie King, founder of New York's New Federal Theatre, believes Perry's characters are much more complex than mere stereotypes. King says, "Tyler goes way beyond the cliches. When Madea is trying to convince a girl to change her life, there's an honesty and brilliance. He taps into that wisdom of our [black] grandmothers and mothers, and we sit there and say, 'Yes.'"[65]

Such criticism once bothered Perry but he came to believe that his characters and plots are worthwhile even though some people do not like them. "With my shows," Perry says, "I try to build a bridge that marries what's deemed legitimate theater and so-called 'chitlin' circuit theater,' and I think I've done pretty well with that, in bringing people in to enjoy a more elevated level of theater."[66] Helping him survive such criticism were famous, influential fans, like Oprah Winfrey. On her daytime television show Winfrey once said, "I saw for the first time the play *Madea Goes to Jail* in Los Angeles. It was a transcendent experience. It was what you want in theater. I laughed so hard … I had a laughing headache."[67]

Even more important than praise from Winfrey was that people kept flocking to Perry's plays. And so he kept writing, directing, producing, and acting in more of them.

A Smart Businessman

From 1998 through 2009, Perry created eleven stage plays, including *Madea's Family Reunion* (2002), *Madea's Class Reunion* (2003), and *Madea Goes to Jail* (2005). Perry worked hard on all his plays, directing and producing them all. The Madea plays were especially tiring for Perry because he was also the star and it was physically demanding to be Madea every night. The fat suit he wears to look

Perry sits in his extravagant $5 million home, nicknamed Avec Chateau, in an Atlanta suburb.

like an overweight, buxom old woman is hot and uncomfortable and makes him sweat profusely. Perry has a smooth, deep-toned voice, and it is difficult for him to talk in Madea's shrill, high-pitched voice several hours a night. Perry explains, "I have to push from the diaphragm to get it. I'm pushing from my diaphragm so I can do it night after night after night after night. That is one of the toughest parts of doing this character, the voice."[68]

Why Tyler Perry Writes Plays

Tyler Perry became rich writing and producing plays. But he wrote the plays because he wanted to provide African Americans with entertainment that they could enjoy and understand because it related to the problems and joys blacks encounter in real life. Perry says,

> It's never been about the money for me. What it is about, in the shows that I do, I speak from the heart about my situations, my life stories. Just we, as African-Americans, never had an outlet for how we deal with things in life, you know, our problems, our issues, our struggles. So I talk about that and all—in my shows and it always goes back to where, you know, church for me, and God, for me, and that's what my shows are about, whatever our problems, our struggles, it's always going to go back to the basics. So when you talk about those things to people who want to hear it, especially in these days when people just need to laugh and have a good time and be lifted up out of, you know, despair, you're going to do well, and that's what's happening right now, and people just want to laugh and get away from the what's happening in the reality of our world.

Tyler Perry, interview by Tavis Smiley, *The Tavis Smiley Show*, National Public Radio, September 9, 2003, www.npr.org/templates/story/story.php?storyId=1424421.

As his success grew, Perry became a shrewd businessman. He produced all of his plays through Tyler Perry Company, a company he started in Atlanta, Georgia. Unlike some playwrights, Perry retained control of his work instead of selling rights to other studios. That allowed him to market DVDs of his plays and CDs of their songs; he has sold millions of both and by 2007 his plays on DVD had produced more than $150 million in revenue. Perry also tried to separate himself from other black playwrights by creating an awareness of his name. He did that by placing his name before the title of his plays so people who liked his work would recognize his new productions. "When I started doing plays, there was a 'Mama-I'm-Going-To-The Store' play every week," Perry says. "So I started to have them put my name on the marquee and on the ticket so that people would know this play is different from the other shows."[69] Perry thus created a distinct brand for his plays that helped make him more well known.

Perry's hard work—in addition to writing Perry often toured with his plays 250 days a year—made him a multi-millionaire and he began to enjoy himself. By 2004 he was living in a $5 million home in suburban Atlanta that has a swimming pool with a waterfall, tennis courts, and two prayer gardens. Perry designed the home, which he nicknamed Avec Chateau. *Avec chateau* means "with home" in French, an apt name for a dwelling owned by someone who was once homeless and lived in a small car. His old Hyundai was replaced by a half-dozen cars, including a red Ferrari, a Bentley Azure, a BMW sedan, and a Range Rover. Perry also had plenty of new clothes and over one hundred pairs of shoes.

Perry, is not ashamed of such conspicuous consumption because he feels he earned it by working so hard. Because Perry still vividly remembers how many times his first play failed, he believes his success can help other people realize what they can achieve with God's help if they work hard enough. Perry says, "I wanted [Avec Chateau] to be vast. I wanted to make a statement, not in any grand or boastful way, but to let people know what God can do when you believe. I don't care how low you go, there's an opposite of low, and as low as I went I wanted to go that much higher. And if there was an opposite of homelessness, I wanted to find it."[70]

Perry did not stop working hard once he became rich. In 2009 *Laugh to Keep from Crying*, his eleventh play, earned solid reviews wherever it played, even though Perry did not act in it. The play centers on Grandview Apartments, whose tenants include Floyd, a comical landlord who provides the humor; a single mother trying to cope with two teenage children; a grieving widow; a woman who was a prostitute; and a newlywed white couple. Palmer Williams Jr., who stars as Floyd, says the play's intricate plot and its characters show how Perry has continued to evolve as a playwright. He notes, "[Perry] is always constantly growing as an artist and a writer. People are demanding more so he's giving them more."[71]

No Longer Dreaming

Perry's success has given him more material wealth than he ever thought possible, and he admits it often feels strange to be so rich after being so poor as a child. He is sometimes reminded of the dreams he had when he was young when he sees children peer through the gates at his luxurious home. Perry says, "I was that little boy walking by looking in and now I'm the person looking out at them, wondering about their dreams."[72]

Chapter 4

A Movie Star

Tyler Perry sometimes talks to theatergoers after his plays end. When the trim, handsome Perry would come onstage after taking off Madea's wig, glasses, and fat suit, the audience would go crazy, clapping and cheering. But after a 2005 performance of *Madea Goes to Jail* at Atlanta's Fox Theatre, Perry had some bad news for his fans. He announced, "*Madea Goes to Jail* is going to be the last tour for Madea. Because . . . we're doing more movies so you guys can see more of Madea on film, because it takes so long for us to get across the country. It takes like sixteen months for us to do a complete tour and then there are a lot of cities saying 'Why didn't you come here, why didn't you come here.'"[73]

Perry made his announcement not long after his first film, *Diary of a Mad Black Woman*, was released on February 25, 2005, and became a hit. Perry knew that making his plays into films would bring them to a much wider audience, and he wanted to reach as many people as he could with the spiritual messages that were such an important part of them. Perry discovered that taking them from the stage to the screen was harder than he thought it would be.

From the Stage to the Screen

Perry went to California in 2002 to talk for the first time with executives of movie studios about his plays. He had already made $150 million from his stage productions and believed his fans and other people would flock to movie theaters to see them as movies. But studio officials doubted there was enough interest in his work and one executive with Paramount Pictures bluntly told Perry, "Black people who go to church don't go to the movies."[74] Another problem Perry encountered was that movie executives wanted control over the movies they financed and filmed, including the power to select the director and the actors and to rewrite scripts. Perry was unwilling to surrender artistic control of his plays because he feared studios would weaken or eliminate his spiritual messages.

Perry was unable to reach an agreement on a film despite meeting with executives of several major movie studios. Because Perry had already been successful selling filmed versions of his stage plays, he began to believe that his best option was to make a movie himself and market it directly to the public. But before he did that, Perry contacted Lionsgate, a relatively new independent firm that produced and distributed films that major studios had rejected, and it was willing to take a chance on Perry. "When they offered me creative control, I was in,"[75] Perry says.

Lionsgate and Perry agreed that Perry would finance half the $5 million needed to make his first movie. Perry gladly put up $2.5 million of his own money because he knew part ownership of the film would guarantee that he had the power to make the movie his way. Perry explains, "He who has the gold makes the rules. If somebody else is gonna give you the money, then, they're gonna be in control. They're gonna own it, they're gonna tell you how it goes. They're gonna give you notes and give you changes. I wasn't willing to do that, so there was no other option for me."[76]

And for Perry, making his first movie proved to be another learning experience.

The First Film

The first play Perry brought to the screen was *Diary of a Mad Black Woman*, the story of what happens to Helen after her husband, Charles, dumps her for another woman. Perry did not direct the film, but he wrote the script, making many changes in the movie version of his play. Perry knew he needed to appeal to people beyond his base of middle-class African American churchgoers. He says, "I didn't lose my core audience, or forget how they want

*Perry's first movie was **Diary of a Mad Black Woman,** released in 2005.*

me to tell the story, but I was also mindful to keep the story universal, so that no matter where you come from, or what your race is, you can relate to it."[77]

Like the play, the movie is about how Helen deals with being deserted by her husband, Charles. She discovers she can survive on her own, falls in love with a man named Orlando, and even helps Charles recover physically after he is shot and left paralyzed. Perry added a second major story line about Brian, a lawyer whose wife left him and their children because she is a drug addict. Both plots end happily; Brian's wife, free from drugs, returns to him in a joyous church scene in which everyone is singing, and the movie closes with Helen agreeing to marry Orlando. The movie maintains the themes of the play, such as the need to forgive people when they hurt you, the strength people in trouble receive from God, and the ability people have to change their lives for the better.

Popular with Women

Tyler Perry's movies are popular with women. Women like his movies because they have female characters who are able to overcome the same problems that women face in real life, such as a husband who cheats. Many of the women in Perry's plays are strong emotionally and they hold their families together. Madea, for all of her comic traits, is one of those women, and the fact that Perry is able to portray her so realistically shows how much he understands women. Perry claims he learned a lot about women when he was a child by spending so much time with his mother, Maxine; his bible-quoting grandmother; and other female relatives. Perry also prefers writing about women because he finds them more interesting than men. He explains, "Women are usually the center of everything in the household. You don't say, 'I'm going to my grandfather's house; you say I'm going to my grandmother's house.' Growing up on my mother's hip, I learned a great deal about women. They have so many colors and so many shades. They can be so much more vulnerable than men. Women are the richest characters to write."

Quoted in Dan Ewald, "From Misery to Mastery," *Christianity Today*, September 10, 2008, www.christianitytoday.com/ct/movies/interviews/2008/tylerperry.html.

The movie also had another vital component of Perry's plays—Madea. Helen is Madea's granddaughter, and she moves in with Madea after Charles throws her out of their palatial home. Madea is surprised Helen is not angrier at the woman who stole her husband and is content to let her get away with it. "No, you gonna deal with him like a white woman. I gonna deal with him like a black woman,"[78] Madea says as she holds her purse, which everyone knows contains a gun. In one of the movie's most hilarious scenes, Madea goes crazy with a chainsaw and destroys much of Charles's house when Madea and Helen go there to get Helen's personal possessions. Perry plays not only Madea but also Brian, who is her nephew, and Joe, her crazy brother.

The movie helped introduce millions of people to Madea, who was unknown to anyone who had not see Perry's plays. Perry was confident that Madea and the film would be popular but he continued touring with the stage version of *Madea Goes to Jail* while the movie was being finished, and he appealed to people in the audience to go see it. He said,

> [Movie executives] told me that black folk who go to church don't go to movies. And they obviously don't know no black people. So, when the movie comes out I want you to go out see it in record numbers. [Prove to the movie executives] that if you give us something we want to see we will see it. And I promise you will not be disappointed.[79]

Defying the Critics

Movie critics often review films before they are released to the public. Many critics savaged *Diary of a Mad Black Woman* before the public saw it, including Roger Ebert, a highly respected Chicago critic who claimed, "I've been reviewing movies for a long time, and I can't think of one that more dramatically shoots itself in the foot."[80] But as so often happens, critics failed to recognize an entertaining film that millions of people wanted to see. In its opening weekend in late February 2005, *Diary of a Mad Black Woman* became a surprise hit as it totaled $21.9 million in ticket

Diary of a Mad Black Woman *became the No. 1 movie,*
replacing **Hitch** *which starred Will Smith, left.*

sales, more than four times what it cost to make. The film even
became the nation's number-one movie, replacing *Hitch*, starring
Will Smith, an African American who is one of the world's most
popular movie stars.

The critics who panned the movie failed to discern the elements that would make it popular. One thing the mostly male
critics did not realize was how much the movie would appeal to
women, who sympathized with Helen's plight and agreed with
the advice she got from Madea and other strong women in the
movie. In one scene Helen's mother, played by renowned black
actress Cicely Tyson, tells her daughter she can handle what
happened to her because "you've got the strength God gave us
women to survive."[81]

Although some critics thought Madea was an interesting character, others dismissed Perry as just another black man dressing up as a woman to get laughs, like comedians Flip Wilson and Martin Lawrence. What the critics missed is how funny and uncannily true to his character Perry is when he performs as Madea. Actor Shemar Moore, who plays Orlando, was full of praise for Perry's performance. He says, "Something happens to him when he puts that wig on. Something flips. Tyler's special."[82]

Many critics who knocked the movie claimed its plot was too simplistic or trite, but people who flocked to the movie obviously loved the simple but uplifting stories of redemption and love which were coupled with spiritual messages. Perry is not shy about stressing how important those elements of his work are. He told one reporter, "I want to represent forgiveness and hope and finding a way through a tough situation. I want to be a place of good energy."[83]

The movie defied critics' predictions that it would be a flop. After it drew so many people on its opening weekend, Ebert wrote another column to admit he had underestimated the appeal of Perry's movie. Acknowledging his misjudgment, Ebert writes, "Well, now I know who Tyler Perry is."[84] And for the first time, millions of other people knew who Perry was too.

More Hit Movies

The success of the film version of *Diary of a Mad Black Woman* lifted Perry to a new level of celebrity and stardom. At the time the movie came out, Perry was touring with a play, so he did not realize at first how drastically the movie had altered his life. He recalls, "I stayed on tour all the way until June, so I didn't feel any of what was happening. I just knew when I got back to Atlanta and tried to go to the mall, something had changed. Before, I could always go to the mall, and a few people might recognize me and stop me, but after [the movie came out], there was a lot of pointing and stuff."[85]

Perry wrote, directed, and starred in his second movie 2006's
Madea's Family Reunion.

Inspiration for a Movie

Tyler Perry's 2007 hit movie *Daddy's Little Girls* is a love story about a divorced man struggling to be a good father to his daughters while trying to begin a new relationship with a woman who has a high-powered job. Perry got the idea for the movie's plot from a friend of his who was always on the phone. He explains,

A 2007 billboard for the movie **Tyler Perry's Daddy's Little Girls.**

I was thinking, "Who is this guy talking to all the time? Every time I turn around he's on the phone and he's supposed to be working." And then I found out it's his children. He has these three beautiful daughters. So he was my muse for Monty [the main character in the movie]. He was a guy that grew up in the 'hood [inner city]. I have another friend who is very successful—[she's] in corporate America—who is really, really rich. She was my muse. She was always saying how she can't find a man. So I was thinking, "What if I introduced the two of them?" And I started laughing so hard. I said, "I gotta write this. It would be hilarious."

Quoted in Rebecca Murray, "Behind the Scenes of 'Daddy's Little Girls' with Tyler Perry," February 12, 2007, http://movies.about.com/od/directorinterviews/a/

Happy with the success of *Diary of a Mad Black Woman*, Lionsgate quickly negotiated with Perry to make more movies as quickly as possible. Since Madea had been such an overwhelmingly popular character in Perry's first film, his second film was

Madea's Family Reunion. The film was rushed into production, and when it opened on February 6, 2006, it was number one, with a weekend total of $30 million in ticket sales. Perry not only starred in the movie, but he also wrote the script and directed the movie. It was the first time Perry directed a movie and he thought he did poorly. He says, "*Madea's Family Reunion* was the worst directing."[86] Lionsgate, however, let him continue directing movies. In reviewing Perry's next film, *Daddy's Little Girls* (2007), newspaper critic Roger Moore praised him for doing a much better job: "[Perry has] gotten comfortable behind the camera. And without Madea, his obese, smart-mouthed alter-ego auntie, to portray, the man in the dress shows he really can direct. [You would] swear the guy took time off to do film school."[87]

Perry continued to have success with his movies, and any movie that had Madea in it was a big hit. When *Madea Goes to Jail* was released on June 16, 2009, ticket sales during its opening weekend totaled $41.1 million, which made it the nation's number-one movie and Perry's biggest opening ever. Steve Rothenberg, Lionsgate's president of distribution, claimed that Perry's comical creation was now so popular with moviegoers that "you could argue that Madea is now the top female box office star in Hollywood. The character is one of the great screen creations of the last decade."[88]

Madea was wildly popular with the public and so were Perry's movies. And admirers of both Perry and his funniest creation were no longer just African Americans.

Widening Appeal

In 2008 the film *The Family That Preys* came out, starring Academy Award–winning white actress Kathy Bates and acclaimed black actress Alfre Woodard. Bates and Woodard play best friends who take a road trip in a vintage turquoise Cadillac to get away from family problems. Perry's decision to cast a white actress in a starring role seemed by many as an attempt to lure more whites to his work. In reviewing the film, *New York Times* critic Stephen Holden notes that it was "a movie that carefully balances its moral and racial equations."[89] The movie may have attracted more whites,

Perry directed Oscar-winning actress Kathy Bates, left, in 2008's The Family That Preys, *about two women who go on a road trip to escape family problems.*

but its opening weekend box office take of $17 million, while successful, was the lowest a Perry movie had ever earned. Meanwhile, ticket sales for Perry's previous movies with only African American actors were so high, it seemed that he must have been drawing white audiences. Reuben Cannon, who helps produce Perry's movies, questioned members of an all-white audience in Sacramento, California, about *Madea's Family Reunion*. He says the white audience liked the film and identified with its values, which stresses marital fidelity, helping family members, and the need not to let money dominate a person's life.

Actor David Mann has been a part of Perry's success since he began appearing in his plays as Madea's obnoxious neighbor, Mr. Brown. Mann has since gone on to star in Perry's movies, including *Meet the Browns* in 2008, and in the television show *Meet the Browns*. Mann has seen Perry's appeal continue to widen since he began acting in his plays on the Urban Theater Circuit before nearly all-black audiences. He says, "I can recall when we first started, I would say 90 to 95 percent of the audience would be African American. But now, you look out there [in the audience] and it's like, 'Wow! It's just a rainbow.'"[90]

Perry himself says he never worries about whether whites will understand his work. He explains, "I believe if you stay true to what you do, eventually everybody will see these are universal stories."[91] However, as audiences for his plays and movies have grown and changed, Perry has been forced to exercise more caution in his creations. An example is Madea's penchant for pulling guns out of her purse and firing them. Even though Madea never shoots anyone, Perry has realized that the message it sends is that shooting a gun in anger is acceptable and it could negatively affect children. Perry had an encounter with a fan that made him realize that he needs to take more care with his characters. He recalls,

> I had a little boy, a six-year-old boy walk up to me, and he pointed his fingers at me as if they were a gun and he said, "Rock-a-bye-baby," which is a line I did in one of the plays, and he starts shooting me. And I thought to myself, it's like, "Tyler, everybody's paying attention, so you really need to [take] responsibility to try and be more careful at what this character was doing."[92]

Perry's new mass appeal also led him to consider whether to leave a scene in his play *Madea's Family Reunion* in which he humorously spanks a child. He tackled the problem by asking the audience after each performance what they thought about Madea spanking a child. When Perry got an overwhelming response not to cut the scene from about thirty thousand people who saw the play in one week, he honored their wishes and left the scene in the play.

"Madea!"

As Perry's fame grew, more people began to recognize him in public. Being recognized by fans is flattering but it can also lead to some strange situations. Because Madea is by far the most popular character Perry has created, many of his fans identify him

Fans identify Perry closely with his character Madea and often yell "Madea" when they see him in person.

closely with her, and when they see him, they yell "Madea!" at him because they love that character so much. Perry admits that he was uncomfortable at first but has since come to understand why fans do it. He says, "When somebody walks up to you and just starts laughing, they can't even concentrate—they're laughing so hard. It used to bother me, but then I realized: 'You bring them joy. When they see you, that's what they feel—joy.'"[93]

Chapter 5

A Movie and Television Mogul

October 4, 2008, was one of the happiest days of Tyler Perry's life. On that day he opened Tyler Perry Studios, a 200,000-square-foot (18,580sq. m) complex on 30 acres (12ha) of land in Atlanta, Georgia, with ample room for business offices and television and movie sets. Perry was ecstatic because he was making history as the first African American to own his own studio. That night he smiled broadly at his parents and crowed, "Look what your baby boy has done."[94] On hand for the gala opening was a star-studded crowd of three hundred that included talk-show host Oprah Winfrey and actors Sidney Poitier and Will Smith. Even Smith, perhaps the world's most popular actor, was in awe of how much Perry had accomplished. "This is an American first, and the first in the universe," Smith said of Perry's studio. "He is not letting anyone get in his way. It's big."[95]

The studio made Perry a powerful player in two fields of entertainment—film and television—that only decades earlier had limited African American participation at nearly all levels of production from acting to operating cameras. Perry was now a business executive with the power to create whatever type of entertainment he wanted in any medium. And Perry gleefully notes that he can hire anyone he wants: "I hired 300 people. A lot of them are African American and people who haven't been able to get jobs in Hollywood, people who haven't been able to get in. They've been able to come here and make a great living, so it's really fantastic."[96]

Tyler Perry attends the opening of Tyler Perry Studios in Atlanta on October 4, 2008.

Creating a Television Show

After Perry's movies began drawing huge audiences, a television network approached him about creating a television series. But when Perry began discussing a show, he ran into the same resistance to his Christian-based messages that he did when he talked to movie studio executives about filming

Tyler Perry's House of Payne, *about an Atlanta fireman forced to move in with his parents, became a huge hit on TBS.*

his plays. Perry was stunned when he was told that characters on television could not talk openly about religion. He discussed it with fans in 2004 after a performance of his play *Meet the Browns*:

> Did you know you can't say "Jesus" in a sitcom? They told me that, and I was like, "You gotta be kiddin' me." If you don't want my God here, you don't want me here either. God has been too good to me to go and try to sell out to get some money. That's O.K. I will sit in a corner and be broke with the Lord before I will sit there and have them give me millions and sell my soul. It ain't gonna happen.[97]

People in the audience applauded Perry for his stand. To ensure that he would have absolute control over what he created, Perry spent $5 million to make ten test episodes of *Tyler Perry's House of Payne*. The show is about an Atlanta, Georgia, fireman who is forced to move in with his parents when his home burns down. The characters are similar to many of those in Perry's plays, as are their problems, which they solve in typical Perry fashion with the help of loving family and friends and faith in God.

Beginning on June 21, 2006, the test episodes ran on selected stations in ten major cities. Just two months later, on August 23, cable television station TBS announced it was buying one hundred new episodes of the show for about $200 million, an unprecedented financial commitment to a new series. The network's faith in Perry was rewarded on June 6, 2007, when the first episode of the series on TBS drew 5.5 million viewers, a record audience for the premiere of a basic-cable original situation comedy. Although many viewers tuned in to see Perry making a guest star appearance as Madea, the show drew a respectable 3.2 million viewers the next week without him.

Debmar-Mercury, an entertainment company, helped Perry distribute the show's test episodes to television stations and strike a deal with TBS. Mort Marcus, copresident of Debmar-Mercury, says Perry succeeded because he was willing to risk his own money to develop a show instead of having a network finance it, which is the way most shows are created. Marcus explains, "The [entertainment] business is changing in general in a lot of ways, and someone like Tyler is very entrepreneurial and would like to control his destiny. He just knew he wanted to create this sitcom and he didn't want to be at the mercy of the networks."[98]

A desire to do things differently has marked Perry's entire career. It is also a major reason why he has been so successful in so many different types of entertainment.

A Hands-On Boss

Something else that has made Perry successful is his strong work ethic, and he participates as much as possible in everything he creates. Despite long hours, Perry writes and directs television shows at the same time he is working on movies and plays, which have remained popular. His hands-on approach extends to making sure that the people who work for him have the same dedication to doing their jobs.

Perry directing film legend Cicely Tyson in 2006. Perry expects his actors and employees to work hard.

Perry's Web Site

Tyler Perry uses his Web site (www.tylerperry.com) to communicate directly with fans. People can sign up to get e-mails from him. In his e-mails, Perry writes about how he feels and about things that are happening to him. The site also archives fan responses to his e-mails.

The saddest e-mail Perry sent was a brief one on December 8, 2009. It read, "Willie Maxine Perry February 12, 1945–December 8, 2009. Thank you for all your prayers." The message, which included a picture of Perry and his mother, was his way of telling his fans that his mother had died. In an emotional e-mail on December 26, Perry explains that he had been at his mother's side almost full time for months before she died. He writes,

> A few months ago, I said I was taking off the rest of 2009. The reason for that, although I didn't say it at the time, was so I could spend my mother's final days at her side. I am so glad I did. It made all the difference in the world to me. Thank you for all of your condolences. As you know, my mother was the apple of my eye, so this has been difficult to say the least. I'll say more about her as I am able. It's just too soon to talk publicly about it. It is still very raw. All I'll say is this, take care of your mothers … you only get one. I've got to stop talking about this, sorry.

Tyler Perry, "Thank You!" TylerPerry.com, December 26, 2009, www.tylerprry.com/_Messages.

Roger Bobb, Perry's supervising producer, says Perry expects his employees to work hard and not make any mistakes. But Bobb also notes that Perry treats his workers fairly: "Tyler Perry is a tornado, but he's also like your brother, and you want him to succeed, so you just don't think about how impossible it all is. Because if you did, you'd have to stop."[99] One example of the impossible demands Perry makes on his employees is the filming schedule for the ten test episodes of *House of Payne*. The episodes were shot in only seventeen days, even though it usually takes a week to shoot just one episode of a half-hour television show.

Perry also demands respect from his employees and demands that they address him as "Mr. Perry" at the studio. But despite his success, Perry is not respected by everyone. Those with negative views of what Perry has accomplished include television and movie critics and even some fellow African American actors and directors.

Perry's Critics

Todd Boyd, a University of Southern California film professor, is highly regarded for his views on black culture and how blacks are represented in the media. In 2009 Boyd told a reporter that the plots of Perry's movies and some of his characters perpetuate stereotypes about uneducated blacks who are unable to control their lives. He said, "It seems a bit ironic that at the moment of the first African-American president [U.S. president Barack Obama], the most popular African-American figure in the media is a man in drag [Perry as Madea] engaging some of the most stereotypical images of African-Americans ever created."[100]

Another harsh critic is Spike Lee, a director, producer, writer, and actor who is highly acclaimed for his movies which deal with serious social issues, like race relations. Lee attacked Perry's work in May 2009 during the Black Enterprise Entrepreneurs Conference in Detroit, Michigan. In remarks aimed at Perry, Lee said, "Each artist should be allowed to pursue their artistic endeavors but I still think there is a lot of stuff out today that is 'coonery' [negatively depicting black people] and buffoonery. I know it's making a lot of money and breaking records, but we can do better."[101]

Television critics have been no kinder. Even though *House of Payne* premiered to a record-setting audience in 2007, critic Robert Bianco blasted the show in his review in the newspaper

What Drives Tyler Perry

In 2006 Tyler Perry's *Don't Make a Black Woman Take Off Her Earrings: Madea's Uninhibited Commentaries on Love and Life* became a best-selling book. In it Mabel "Madea" Simmons, Perry's most famous character, uses her trademark humor mixed with wisdom to discuss a wide variety of topics. In the book's conclusion, Perry discusses his own life, and explains what drives him to keep creating plays, movies, and television shows. He writes,

> Do you know it's awesome to have people come up to me and say, "Thanks for telling my story…. Thanks for letting me see me…. Thanks for letting me know what I need to do for this situation." It is an experience that is surreal and overwhelming. But it also lets me know that I am where I'm supposed to be in this life. I give praise to God every day for it. What rings true is that everything we go through in life will work for our good. One day I realize that all the things that I have endured were for the benefit of helping potentially millions of other people, helping us to laugh through this life. That is the amazing and powerful gift from which I draw strength to go on to the next thing.

Tyler Perry, *Don't Make a Black Woman Take Off Her Earrings: Madea's Uninhibited Commentaries on Love and Life*, New York: Riverhead Books, 2006, p. 252.

USA Today. Under the headline "House of Payne: It Hurts to Watch," Bianco claims the show "isn't just the worst sitcom of the year, it's one of the worst of the modern era."[102] Bianco criticized the writing, saying the jokes were old and not very funny, and wrote that the characters were not much fun to watch. Linda Armstrong, a television critic for the *New York Amsterdam News* newspaper, wrote in her review that she liked Perry's previous work, but she ridiculed *House of Payne* and said Perry needed to make a lot of changes to make it a success.

Yet *House of Payne* was a hit, and Perry's defenders claim that his critics fail to realize how attuned Perry is to providing entertainment that his African American target audience enjoys. Actor Blair Underwood, who stars in *Madea's Family Reunion*, explains why Perry's work is so popular: "He says things, and in ways, that especially in the black community, we understand exactly what he's saying, because we've heard those things since childhood."[103]

For the most part, Perry ignores his critics because his continuing success is his best argument against them.

Perry's Life Today

In December 2008 Perry and a reporter visited the small, dingy, one-room Atlanta apartment he lived in before his first play became a success in 1998. Perry told the reporter he had been glad to have the apartment after being homeless for several months and that he never wants to forget "how close I came to losing everything" while pursuing his dream. Perry then pointed to different areas of the apartment and explained, "My bed was there. My stove was there.... That little corner there, that's where my computer sat. That's where I ran from my fears [by writing]."[104]

Perry kept writing about his fears, thoughts, and other emotions, and those words became the essence of his plays, movies, television shows, and even a best-selling book—*Don't Make a Black Woman Take Off Her Earrings: Madea's Uninhibited Commentaries on Love and Life*—that have lifted him out of a lonely life of poverty. A decade after barely surviving in that apartment, Perry was living in a luxurious mansion in an exclusive Atlanta suburb. Perry also has a home in Los Angeles, California, but he continues to reside in Atlanta and do most of his work there. He says he could never live in Hollywood, the movie capital in Los Angeles, because of the obsession so many people there have with fame, money, and prestige.

But even living in Atlanta has not allowed Perry to get away from the problems of being a wealthy celebrity. In February 2009, Perry obtained a restraining order against a woman who had been sending

Perry's book Don't Make a Black Woman Take Off Her Earrings *was released in 2006 and became a best-seller.*

him threatening e-mails and even showed up at his Atlanta studios. Even though his mansion is surrounded by a high fence, fans have managed to get over it and leave messages on his doorstep. Like many other celebrities, Perry has discovered that fame and fortune has a negative side. He admits, "When you get to a level of success, you deal with a lot of things you weren't expecting."[105]

The insincerity some people display toward celebrities and their greedy desire to use them for their own purposes has even affected Perry's personal relationships. One of Perry's first serious girlfriends was a woman he met in a club in Atlanta. He pursued her for several years, and after he became successful, he bought her a new car. Perry was shocked by the woman's disparaging attitude toward his generous gift. He recalls, "Afterward she called me up and asked me, 'Would you drive this?'"[106] Realizing the woman only liked him because of his money and fame, Perry quit seeing her and gave the car to his sister.

Not much is known about Perry's personal life because he is a very private person who does not talk to the news media about personal things, like who he is dating. The lack of stories about girlfriends and the fact that Perry dresses up as a woman to play his most famous character led to rumors he might be gay. Perry laughs off such claims, saying it is not his problem that some people cannot separate him from a character he invented. However, Perry has been linked to female celebrities, like former model and talk-show host Tyra Banks, and in 2009 he was dating model Gelila Bekele. Perry freely admits that his celebrity status complicates his relationships with women: "Relationships are tough. Then you add fame and money on top of that. Then people and tabloids and gossip and blogs—put all of that stuff on top—it's tough."[107]

Perry has said for years that he wants to marry and have children. Unfortunately, he has been so busy that meeting someone who could become his wife has been difficult. But one thing Perry has found time to do is to help other people with the vast amounts of money he has made. On November 23, 2009, the National Association for the Advancement of Colored People (NAACP), a civil rights organization, announced that it had received a $1 million donation from Perry. It was the largest, single gift ever given to the NAACP by an individual. Perry says he donated the money to the NAACP because it had helped him and other African Americans to succeed in life by working to ensure their equality with whites. It was the second million-dollar charitable donation Perry ever made.

A Girl Named Precious

One of the most acclaimed movies of 2009 was *Precious*, the story of an African American girl named Precious who is mentally, physically, and sexually abused by her parents. Perry thought the movie was so important that he agreed to be an executive producer; he knew that his involve-

The cast of the movie Precious, *executive produced by Tyler Perry and Oprah Winfrey.*

ment would generate publicity to help make it successful. He also persuaded Oprah Winfrey to be an executive producer of the movie. Perry explains the film's significance below:

> This story [of such abuse] has not been told yet and it is still going on. It is still present in our society and I think that somebody had to do it. I am so glad that [director] Lee Daniels [made the movie] and I just wanted to support [it].... [Mary, Precious's mother] is [just like] my father, so I know it well. They [child abusers] can exist and they are real. What it did for me as I was watching the film and I got to the end of it, I felt such relief, such a weight off of me because I made it, and that is what I think people who have been through it [will feel]. When they see it, they are going to be like, wow. I made it through. That is what is so powerful about it.

Quoted in Alicia Quarles, "Winfrey, Perry Team Up To Promote 'Precious,'" *Seattle Pilot*,

Perry was once rumored to have dated model/TV host Tyra Banks. He is very private and keeps his relationships out of the public eye.

The first was to victims of Hurricane Katrina, the 2005 storm that devastated his hometown of New Orleans. After taping the play *Madea Goes to Jail* in 2006, Perry talked to the audience about the donation. He said, "I have given a million dollars to help rebuild the lower Ninth Ward [a poor black section of New Orleans devastated by Katrina]. I wanted to tell you that [because] every dime that you guys have ever invested in me allowed me to do this. If you bought anything Tyler Perry, you are the person who helped me do this. So, thank you for that."[108]

Perry has made many smaller donations, including fifty thousand each to the Atlanta Community Food Bank and the Hosea Feed the Hungry and Homeless funds in Atlanta in November 2009. In August 2009 he also treated sixty-five children from a Philadelphia, Pennsylvania, day-care center to a trip to Disney World in Orlando, Florida. Perry felt sorry for the children after a Philadelphia swimming club backed out of a deal to let them use its pool because most of the children were black. Perry, who met with the kids at Disney World, said he donated the money because "I want them to know that for every act of evil that a few people will throw at you, there are millions more who will do something kind for them."[109]

Helping people see the goodness that resides in other people is something Perry has always tried to do through his plays, movies, and television shows. For his efforts Perry has won many awards, including the 2010 NAACP Image Award Chairman Award.

Perry's Future

Despite all that Perry had accomplished by 2009, he has an even bigger dream for the future: He wants to control an entire television network. Perry wants to start his own network so he can provide even more entertainment mixed with moral and Christian messages of hope and faith to his fans. He says, "I'd like to have a network where the longer you watch it, the more inspired you get."[110] Perry admits that his unending creative urge forces him to keep working. He says, "I wish I could turn it off for a few hours every now and then. But I would never complain about it, because it's a great gift and a great blessing, and if I didn't have it, I don't know where I'd be."[111]

Perry believes he must use his talents because they are gifts from God. Perry also believes that everyone has some sort of

Tyler Perry accepting the Chairman's Award at the 41st NAACP Image Awards in February 2010.

talent that they can use to make their life better. He explains, "Do everything you can. Whatever your gift is and it's given to you no matter what's going on in the world, no matter how many singers, no matter how many writers, your gift will make room for you in that situation. So, I always believe that. If it's your gift nurture it and make it the best that it can be."[112]

Introduction: A Man of Many Talents

1. Tyler Perry, "Featurette: Tyler Perry Commentary," *Diary of a Mad Black Woman* (movie), DVD, directed by Tyler Perry. Santa Monica, CA: Lionsgate Home Entertainment, 2005.
2. Tyler Perry, "Tyler Perry's I Know I've Been Changed," souvenir booklet. Atlanta, GA: Solstice Group and Child's Entertainment, 2000.
3. Quoted in Kenneth Miles and Robyn D. Clarke, "From the Streets to the Stage," *Black Enterprise*, March 2001, p. 113.
4. Quoted in Pamela K. Johnson, "Diary of a Brilliant Black Man," *Essence*, March 2006, p. 122.

Chapter 1: A Difficult Childhood

5. Quoted in Byron Pitts, "He Is One of America's Top Filmmakers, Yet Few Have Ever Heard of Him," *60 Minutes*, CBS, October 22, 2009, www.cbsnews.com/stories/2009/10/22/60minutes/main5410095.shtml.
6. Quoted in *Conversations Magazine*, "Tyler Perry Interview," AuthorDen.com, 2006, www.authorsden.com/categories/article_top.asp?catid=30&id=21900.
7. Tyler Perry, "We're All Precious in His Sight," TylerPerry.com, March 3, 2009, www.tylerperry.com/_Messages.
8. Tyler Perry, "Forgiving My Father," *Essence*, September 2004, p. 150.
9. Quoted in DeNeen L. Brown, "Madea Goes to Town," *Washington Post*, February 24, 2006.
10. Perry, "Forgiving My Father," p. 150.
11. Quoted in Jamie Foster Brown, "Tyler Perry: On Another Level," *Sister2Sister*, April 2006, www.mahoganycafe.com/tylerperry.html.
12. Quoted in Dan Ewald, "From Misery to Mastery," *Christianity Today*, September 10, 2008, www.christianitytoday.com/movies/interviews/2008/tylerperry.html.

13. Quoted in Brown, "Tyler Perry."
14. Quoted in Brown, "Madea Goes to Town."
15. Perry, "We're All Precious in His Sight."
16. Quoted in Scott Bowles, "Perry Holds on to His Past," *USA Today*, September 10, 2008.
17. Quoted in Phil Kloer, "Frankly, Madea, Tyler Perry's Appeal Is Universal," *Atlanta Journal-Constitution*, February 22, 2006, www.austin360.com/movies/content/movies/stories/2006/02/23perry.html.
18. Quoted in Nicole Symmonds, "Film Director Tyler Perry Strives To Inspire, Motivate," *State Journal-Register*, October 4, 2009, www.sj-r.com/features/x1128391735/Film-director-Tyler-Perry-strives-to-inspire-motivate.
19. Tyler Perry, "The End of Fury," *O, The Oprah Magazine*, March 2006, www.oprah.com/article/omagazine/aha/rys_omag_200603_aha/3.
20. Quoted in Pitts, "He Is One of America's Top Filmmakers."
21. Quoted in Pitts, "He Is One of America's Top Filmmakers."
22. Quoted in Nadira A. Hira, "Diary of a Mad Businessman," *Fortune*, February 19, 2007, p. 84.
23. Quoted in Lorenza Munoz, "The Hollywood Gospel According to Tyler Perry," *Los Angeles Times*, February 19, 2006, http://articles.latimes.com/2006/feb/19/business/fi-tylerperry19.
24. Quoted in Margena A. Christian, "Becoming Tyler: Bill Collector Turned Billion-Dollar Media Mogul Was Molded from Pain, Promise and Persistence," *Ebony*, October 2008, p. 4.
25. Quoted in Kloer, "Frankly, Madea, Tyler Perry's Appeal Is Universal."
26. Perry, "Forgiving My Father," p. 150.
27. Quoted in Ewald, "From Misery to Mastery."
28. Maxine Perry, "Featurette: Tyler Perry Commentary," *Diary of a Mad Black Woman* (movie).
29. Quoted in Lena Williams, "At Home With: Tyler Perry; God Must Love Gilt," *New York Times*, July 8, 2004.
30. Perry, "Forgiving My Father."
31. Quoted in Jeanne Wolf, "Oprah Winfrey and Tyler Perry Say: 'Have Faith in Something Big,'" *Parade Magazine*,

October 25, 2009, www.parade.com/celebrity/2009/10/oprah-winfrey-tyler-perry-have-faith.html.

32. Quoted in Karen Grigsby Bates, "Playwright Perry Takes 'Mad Black Woman' to the Screen," *Day to Day*, National Public Radio, February 25, 2005, www.npr.org/templates/story/story.php?storyId=4513426.

Chapter 2: A Play with a Message

33. Quoted in Susan Horsburgh, "From Rags to Riches," *People*, August 9, 2004, p. 101.

34. Quoted in Bates, "Playwright Perry Takes 'Mad Black Woman' to the Screen."

35. Quoted in Marcia A. Cole, "That's 'Madea,' Honey, Not 'Medea,' and It's a Long Way from Tragedy," *New York Times*, May 5, 2005.

36. Quoted in Hira, "Diary of a Mad Businessman," p. 76.

37. Quoted in Kloer, "Frankly, Madea, Tyler Perry's Appeal Is Universal."

38. Quoted in Tom Waits, "Lord, I Know I've Been Changed," song, composed by Bruce More. Santa Barbara, CA: Santa Barbara Music Publishing, www.lyricsmania.com/lyrics/tom_waits_lyrics_2575/orphans__brawlers_lyrics_33791/lord_ive_been_changed_lyrics_365710.html.

39. Quoted in Bonga Percy Vilakazi, "Talented Tyler," *True Love*, April 2009, p. 24.

40. Quoted in *Conversations Magazine*, "Tyler Perry Interview."

41. Quoted in Vilakazi, "Talented Tyler," p. 24.

42. Perry, "Featurette: Tyler Perry Commentary," *Diary of a Mad Black Woman* (movie).

43. Quoted in Kristi Watts, "The 700 Club with Pat Robertson: The Many Faces of Tyler Perry," 700 Club, www.cbn.com/700club/guests/interviews/tyler_perry050906.aspx.

44. Quoted in Margena A. Christian, "Tyler Perry: Meet the Man Behind the Urban Theater Character Madea," *Jet*, December 1, 2003, p. 62.

45. Quoted in Johnson, "Diary of a Brilliant Black Man," p. 120.

46. Quoted in Ewald, "From Misery to Mastery."

47. Quoted in Watts, "The 700 Club with Pat Robertson."

48. Quoted in Watts, "The 700 Club with Pat Robertson."

49. Quoted in Ton Kennedy "Change Is Good in 'I Know I've Been Changed,'" *Alestle*, November 30, 1999, www.siue. edu/ALESTLE/library/fall99/nov.30/change.html.

50. Quoted in Bowles, "Perry Holds on to His Past."

51. Quoted in Vilakazi, "Talented Tyler," p. 25.

52. Quoted in Zondra Hughes, "How Tyler Perry Rose from Homelessness to a $5 Million Mansion," *Ebony*, January 2004, p. 44.

Chapter 3: A Successful Playwright

53. Quoted in Cole, "That's 'Madea,' Honey, Not 'Medea,' And It's a Long Way From Tragedy."

54. Quoted in Pitts, "He Is One of America's Top Filmmakers."

55. Quoted in Johnson, "Diary of a Brilliant Black Man," p. 120.

56. *Tyler Perry's I Can Do Bad All by Myself*, DVD, directed by Tyler Perry. Atlanta, GA: Tyler Perry Company, 2005.

57. *Tyler Perry's I Can Do Bad All by Myself*.

58. Quoted in Lisa Rose, "The Unlikely Mogul: Tyler Perry Dishes on New Film, His Critics, and His Faith," *Black Christian News*, September 2009, http://blackchristiannews.com/ news/2009/09/the-unlikely-mogul-tyler-perry-dishes-on-new-film-his-critics-and-his-faith.html.

59. Tyler Perry, "Scene Commentary," *Tyler Perry's I Can Do Bad All by Myself*.

60. Quoted in C. Bottomley, "Tyler Perry: Maker of a Mad Black Woman," VH1, March 1, 2005, www.vh1.com/movies/person/ 364367/news/articles/1497593/feature.jhtml.

61. *Meet the Browns* (play), DVD, directed by Tyler Perry. Santa Monica, CA: Lionsgate Home Entertainment, 2005.

62. *Meet the Browns* (play).

63. Quoted in Munoz, "The Hollywood Gospel According to Tyler Perry."

64. Quoted in Pitts, "He Is One of America's Top Filmmakers."

65. Quoted in Russell Scott Smith, "The New Amos 'n' Andy?" Salon.com, February 23, 2006, www.salon.com/ent/feature/ 2006/02/23/perry.

66. Quoted in *Conversations Magazine*, "Tyler Perry Interview."
67. Quoted in Brown, "Madea Goes to Town."
68. Perry, "Scene Commentary," *I Can Do Bad All by Myself*.
69. Quoted in Christian, "Becoming Tyler," p. 4.
70. Quoted in Hughes, "How Tyler Perry Rose from Homelessness to a $5 Million Mansion," p. 44.
71. Quoted in Sara Bauknecht, "Tyler Perry's New Play Is Staged at Petersen Events Center," *Pittsburgh Post-Gazette*, November 05, 2009, www.post-gazette.com/pg/09309/1010807-325.stm.
72. Quoted in Williams, "At Home With: Tyler Perry; God Must Love Gilt."

Chapter 4: A Movie Star

73. Tyler Perry, "Special Features," *Madea Goes to Jail* (play), DVD, directed by Tyler Perry. Santa Monica, CA: Lionsgate Home Entertainment, 2006.
74. Quoted in Munoz, "The Hollywood Gospel According to Tyler Perry."
75. Quoted in Addie Morfoot, "Lionsgate 'Mad' for Perry," *Variety*, February 2005, p. 56.
76. Quoted in Pitts, "He Is One of America's Top Filmmakers."
77. Quoted in Nicole LaPorte, "'Diary' Dear to Lions Gate," *Variety*, July 12, 2004, www.variety.com/article/VR1117907686.html.
78. *Diary of a Mad Black Woman* (play), DVD, directed by Tyler Perry. Santa Monica, CA: Lionsgate Home Entertainment, 2005.
79. *Madea Goes to Jail* (play).
80. Quoted in Brett Pulley, "A Showbiz Whiz," *Forbes*, October 3, 2005, p. 75.
81. *Diary of a Mad Black Woman* (movie).
82. Quoted in Bottomley, "Tyler Perry."
83. Quoted in *USA Today*, "'Mad Black Woman' Puts Tyler Perry on the Map," *USA Today*, March 2, 2005.
84. Quoted in Pulley, "A Showbiz Whiz," p. 75.
85. Quoted in aalbc.com, "Tyler on Madea and More," aalbc.com, http://aalbc.com/reviews/tyler_perry.htm.

86. Quoted in Rebecca Murray, "Behind the Scenes of *Daddy's Little Girls* with Tyler Perry," About.com, February 12, 2007, http://movies.about.com/od/directorinterviews/a/daddys-tp021207.htm.

87. Quoted in Roger Moore, "Daddy's Little Girls," *Orlando Sentinel*, February 14, 2007.

88. Quoted in "King Tyler, Queen Madea," *Jet*, March 16, 2009, p. 29.

89. Quoted in Stephen Holden, "Money Isn't Everything When Values Are at Stake," *New York Times*, September 12, 2008, http://movies.nytimes.com/2008/09/13/movies/13perr.html.

90. Quoted in Alan Duke, "Tyler Perry Is Still Looking for Respect," CNN, February 16, 2009, www.cnn.com/2009/showbiz/movies/02/16/madea.goes.to.europe/index.html#cnnstctext.

91. Quoted in Kloer, "Frankly, Madea, Tyler Perry's Appeal Is Universal."

92. Quoted in Renee Montagne, "Tyler Perry's Impressive Hollywood Rise," *Morning Edition*, National Public Radio, April 24, 2006.

93. Quoted in Bottomley, "Tyler Perry."

Chapter 5: A Movie and Television Mogul

94. Quoted in Cori Murray, "Oh, What a Night!" *Essence*, December 2008, p. 24.

95. Quoted in Isoul H. Harris, "Tyler Perry Makes History and Oprah Is There!" *People*, October 5, 2008, www.people.com/people/article/0,,20231233,00.html?xid=rss-fullcontentcnn.

96. Quoted in Kathy-Ann Joseph, "Tyler Perry," *Essence*, December 2008, p. 153.

97. Quoted in *Time*, "God and Tyler Perry vs. Hollywood," *Time*, March 20, 2008, www.time.com/time/magazine/article/0,9171,1724393,00.html.

98. Quoted in Christopher Lisotta, "House of Payne," *Television Week*, April 17, 2006, p. 27.

99. Quoted in Hira, "Diary of a Mad Businessman," p. 84.

100. Quoted in Andy Segal, "Black in America 2: Perry's Greatest Accomplishment Has Nothing To Do with Business," CNN, July 23, 2009, www.cnn.com/2009/SHOWBIZ/07/23/bia. tyler.perry/index.html.

101. Spike Lee, interview by Ed Gordon, *Black Enterprise*, May 19, 2009, www.blackenterprise.com/television/our-world-with-black-enterprise-television-19/2009/05/30/our-world-episode-73.

102. Robert Bianco, "House of Payne: It Hurts To Watch," *USA Today*, June 5, 2007, www.usatoday.com/life/television/reviews/2007-06-05-house-of-payne_n.html.

103. Quoted in Kloer, "Frankly, Madea, Tyler Perry's Appeal Is Universal."

104. Quoted in Scott Bowles, "Perry Holds on to His Past."

105. Quoted in Kloer, "Frankly, Madea, Tyler Perry's Appeal Is Universal."

106. Quoted in Denene Millner, "The Unstoppable Tyler Perry," *Essence*, August 2007, p. 154.

107. Quoted in Sonia Murray, "The Talented Mr. Perry," *Essence*, February 2009, pp. 112–37.

108. Perry, "Special Features," *Madea Goes to Jail* (play).

109. Quoted in Stephen M. Silverman, "Tyler Perry Sends Snubbed Kids to Disney World," *People*, July 21, 2009, www.people.com/people/article/0,,20292532,00.html.

110. Quoted in Murray, "The Talented Mr. Perry," p. 137.

111. Quoted in Ellen McCarthy, "Tyler Perry's House of Hope," *Washington Post*, March 21, 2008, www.washingtonpost.com/wp-dyn/content/article/2008/03/20/AR2008032001384. html.

112. Quoted in *Conversations Magazine*, "Tyler Perry Interview."

Important Dates

1969

September 14: Tyler Perry is born as Emmitt R. Perry Jr.

1985

Changes his name from Emmitt to Tyler.

1992

Stages the play *I Know I've Been Changed* for the first time in Atlanta, Georgia.

2000

The character of Mabel "Madea" Simmons makes her first appearance in Perry's second play, *I Can Do Bad All by Myself*.

2005

February 25: *Diary of a Mad Black Woman*, Perry's first movie, is released.

2006

February 6: The movie *Madea's Family Reunion* is released.
June 21: Test episodes of the *House of Payne* television show premiere on selected stations.

2007

June 6: *House of Payne* begins airing exclusively on the TBS cable channel.

2008

October 4: Establishes Tyler Perry Studios in Atlanta, Georgia.

2009

January 7: The *Meet the Browns* television show premieres on TBS.
June 16: The movie *Madea Goes to Jail* is released.

For More Information

Books

Amy Fuller, ed., *Contemporary Authors*, vol. 254. Detroit, MI: Thomson Gale, 2007.

Thomas Riggs, ed., *Contemporary Theatre, Film and Television*, vol. 91. Detroit, MI: Cengage Gale, 2009.

Periodicals

Pamela K. Johnson, "Diary of a Brilliant Black Man." *Essence*, March 2006.

Sonia Murray, "The Talented Mr. Perry." *Essence*, February 2009.

Brett Pulley, "A Showbiz Whiz." *Forbes*, October 3, 2005.

Internet Sources

Phil Kloer, "Frankly, Madea, Tyler Perry's Appeal Is Universal." *Atlanta Journal-Constitution*, February 22, 2006, www.austin360.com/movies/content/movies/stories/2006/02/23perry.html.

Byron Pitts, "He Is One of America's Top Filmmakers, Yet Few Have Ever Heard of Him." *60 Minutes*, CBS, October 22, 2009, www.cbsnews.com/stories/2009/10/22/60minutes/main5410095.shtml.

Andy Segal, "Black in America 2: Perry's Greatest Accomplishment Has Nothing To Do with Business." CNN, July 23, 2009, www.cnn.com/2009/SHOWBIZ/07/23/bia.tyler.perry/index.html.

Web Sites

Internet Media Database (http://www.imdb.com/name/nm1347153/). This site includes a page on Tyler Perry that lists information about Perry, his work, photos, and video clips on his plays, movies, and television shows.

TylerPerry.com (www.tylerperry.com). This is Tyler Perry's personal Web site. It includes information about his life as well as his plays, movies, and television shows. It archives e-mails Perry sends to fans and has a message board where fans can leave messages.

Michael V. Uschan has written over seventy books, including *Life of an American Soldier in Iraq*, for which he won the 2005 Council for Wisconsin Writers Juvenile Nonfiction Award. Uschan began his career as a writer and editor with United Press International, a wire service that provided stories to newspapers, radio, and television. Uschan considers writing history books a natural extension of the skills he developed in his many years as a journalist. He and his wife, Barbara, reside in the Milwaukee suburb of Franklin, Wisconsin.